WHICH WAY THE FAMILY ?

Larry Christenson

 DIMENSION BOOKS
Bethany Fellowship, Inc.
Minneapolis, Minn.

WHICH WAY THE FAMILY?

by Larry Christenson

Over the past several years I have had the privilege of speaking to thousands of couples who are searching—sometimes in near desperation—for a better family life. Mothers tearfully relate the lies and deceptions which have come to light with a teenage daughter, or the rebellion of a son seemingly against every kind of adult authority. Fathers shake their heads in puzzlement over the sweet daughter who almost overnight sheds her girlhood innocence for suggestive dress, stringy hair, harsh-looking companions, vulgar talk, and too-easy familiarity with boys. Parents turn up their palms in bewilderment at the unreasonable attitudes and demands of seven- and eight-year-old children—and usually give in to them. Wives complain about the husband who never has time to spend with the family, yet expects her to keep house and children running like a precision clock. Husbands wonder why they should have to battle the world for a living ten and twelve hours a day, then come home and open the door to the clamor of seventeen problems. The husband may stomp and bellow his frustration, while the wife turns hers into nagging, and the children

3

turn theirs into naughtiness or sullen withdrawal. Yet behind these varied reactions stands a single plea: *What can we do?* What can we do to make this thing of family life somehow work better?

The family has gone through stormy waters in times past. It is a sturdy old craft. Storm gales have risen up in our day. Punishing waves are battering the hull of family life. Some alarmists have given out the cry to abandon ship—marriage and the family are going down. But we've sailed too long on this boat. Its tossing, pitching deck is still a better hope than being cast adrift on an uncharted sea. And indeed, marriage and family are designed to ride out the worst of storms and still hang together. But for that a firm hand is needed on the wheel.

When the weather is calm, a ship can plough off course without getting into serious difficulty; other ships, and shore stations, will sound a warning in time to avoid disaster. In times past, the general culture was supportive of marriage and the family. If a man began to veer off course, a sharp warning would be sounded from an employer, concerned and honest friends, the preacher, and assorted members of an extended family, probably including a Dutch uncle or two. But when a storm closes in, reference points become lost. Many of the moral reference points in our society have been swallowed up in a heaving sea of relativism. Storm-tossed and battered, each family is running its course alone. Warnings are drowned out by howling winds of tumult and change. And up on the bridge, the wheel of the ship spins crazily in the storm. No firm hand commands the rudder. The family is being tossed about at the mercy of the storm. For the captain has abandoned his station.

Too many fathers are lounging in the captain's quarters, claiming the privileges of "head of the household," without exercising the responsibilities that go with it. Too many husbands have delegated the responsibility of command and decision to a mate. Too many men have shrunk back from being that symbol of manly courage, unshaken by the storm, from whom a wife and children draw determination and strength. What can we do to make this thing of a family life work better? *Let fathers get back on deck, take the wheel, and set a positive course for their families.* The great cry of the family in our day is for the steady hand of a father, holding to the course, for those whose lives are committed to his care.

Fathers who recognize the distress of their families, and who determine to stand by their responsibility as fathers, will need a radically renewed understanding of what it means to be a father. The present role of the father in the family, and a renewed understanding of what the role must become, can be established in relation to three points of reference. First of all, the model of fatherhood which has been operating in our culture is inadequate. We need a better one. Second, the relationship to one's mate has become clouded with conflict and confusion. It needs to be clearly defined. Third, the direction of family life has become vague and indefinite. A well laid-out map is needed, so that a father can chart his family's course with understanding and confidence. A model . . . a mate . . . a map. These are points of reference around which a renewed understanding of fatherhood can cluster, and from which can issue a new direction for family life.

A MODEL

Some schools of psychology and anthropology tell us that "God" is a projection of the father-image. The idea of an all-wise, all-competent, all-powerful God is simply a grown-up version of the little child's belief that "My Dad can do anything!"

The Bible comes at it the other way around. The idea of God's fatherhood is not built upon the analogy of human fatherhood. Rather, human fatherhood derives its meaning from the fatherhood of God. "When I think of the greatness of this great plan, I fall on my knees before God the

Father (from whom all fatherhood, earthly or heavenly, derives its name)" (Ephesians 3:14-15, Phillips). Human fatherhood is an expression or illustration of God's divine fatherhood.

God's fatherhood is eternal. He is eternally the Father, just as Christ is eternally the Son. He does not become a father because He adopts us as sons, but He adopts us because He already is the eternal Father. The "fatherhood of God" is therefore no mere anthropomorphism, culturally determined, nor is it limited to describing a relationship between God and man. It expresses something of the nature of God, which pre-dates all thought of human fatherhood. It touches on all creation. The all-embracing fatherhood of God is a foundational truth of the Christian faith: "I believe in one God, *the Father Almighty*, Maker of heaven and earth, and of all things visible and invisible." We will never adequately understand or explain human fatherhood if we limit our inquiry to the sphere of human society or culture. For fatherhood is rooted in the eternal nature of God. An understanding of fatherhood must begin with an understanding of God, the eternal Father. He Himself is the model for our human fatherhood.

What kind of father is God? What characterizes His fatherhood? We begin to understand His fatherhood when we see how it operates—just as we might get a grasp of carpentry or machine tooling through learning the principles by which the craftsman works at his trade. How does God work at the business of being Father?

God's fatherhood operates according to a principle which, like His fatherhood, is eternal. It is the principle of headship. He has built the headship principle into the structure of His creation; and with particular reference to family life, "The head of every man is Christ, the head of a woman is her husband, the head of Christ is God" (I Corinthians 11:3). The fatherhood of God projects itself into human life through the principle of headship. To be a father, according to the model of God, is to be a "head."

1. Headship Establishes Direction.

The primary function of headship is to *establish and maintain direction*. Headship plots the ship's course and is responsible to bring it through to its appointed destination. Part of the conflict and confusion which we witness in homes today stems from a too-simplistic understanding and exercise of headship. To be head of the house is more than a man's privilege of occupying the captain's quarters and barking out orders. It means learning to bear the burdens of responsibility for giving the family informed and intelligent leadership. Headship involves a sensitive interplay of three basic components: submission, authority and love.

What kind of word-association would most people come up with for "head of the house"? A lopsided majority would probably blurt out "authority" or a near-equivalent. But "authority" is not the first word for the head of the house. It is pointedly a second word. The first word is submission.

A father first begins to understand his work as head of the family when he recognizes that he himself is under authority, that he is responsible to Someone higher than himself. "The head of every man is Christ." Before a father can fully exercise headship over his family, he must himself come under the headship of Christ. The headship operates within a clearly defined chain-of-command. If the chain is broken at any point, authority breaks down.

A Roman centurion once came to Jesus and asked Him to heal his servant. He believed that Jesus could do this, and his belief was rooted in a penetrating grasp of the principle of authority. "I am a man under authority," he said, "with soldiers under me. I say to one 'Go,' and he goes; and to another,'Come' and he comes". (Matthew 8:9). We might have expected him to say, "I am a man who *has* authority. . . ." But the centurion was much humbler and wiser. He recognized that his authority to command a soldier rested upon the fact that, as a Roman officer, he stood properly lined up in the chain-of-command, his word was equivalent to the word of the Emperor. And he recognized in Jesus a similar exercise of authority in the spiritual realm. The fact that Jesus could command spiritual forces rested upon the fact that He, too, was "under authority," that He was properly lined up in *God's* chain-of-command.

In the same way that Christ's authority was rooted in His submission to God, a father's authority grows out of his submission to Christ. He does not command the ship on his own authority, he does it as one living under the headship of Christ. He does not exercise authority over his wife and children according to personal whim, but according to the word of Christ. A father does not set a course for his family following his own preferences, but he follows the map which is given to him by Christ.

Paradoxically, therefore, the primary focus of a father must not be upon his family, as such, but upon Christ. If he loses his personal focus on Christ, he loses his fundamental standing as a father. He may be concerned. He may expend great effort at being a successful father. But if he is not living under Christ's authority, he is building on sand. Not a few parents focus myopically on their own children, their own family, while neglecting their responsibility to God. When rebellion and discontent show up in the children, they redouble their efforts, but often with little effect. For they are concentrating on the wrong thing first. The children do not need more concern, more attention, more of the family limelight. What they need is the example of a father and others who are living responsibly under the authority of Christ.

A father who is concerned over his son's carelessness in money matters may need to teach him some simple principles of management; teaching children practical issues of life is a normal duty of parents. But the problem may have a deeper root: Is the father responsible *to God* in his own financial affairs? Does he tithe his income? He may be a successful businessman, but if he is resistant to Christ's authority in the area of money, he should not be surprised if his children's financial affairs get fouled up. Our sins and failings, unapparent to the world, often show up in our children.

2. Headship exercises authority.

Authority, the second component of headship, flows naturally from the father's submission to Christ. Because this father is living under Him, Christ is able to entrust to him certain authority over his family. It is not the father's authority, as such, which functions in a Christian home, but it is Christ's authority, operating through the father.

Because it flows from Christ, the authority of a Christian father will manifest the gentleness of Christ. A husband may see that his wife is distracted and irritable with all the clamor of the children at breakfast time—lunches to fix, breakfast to prepare, Janet dashing in with an "emergency!" She needs a shoebox theater for second-hour English class, and Todd forgot to bring his history paper home to be signed, so he begs Mom to drive him to school and sign it so he won't get docked ten points.

That night the father sits down with his family and lays out a plan. Susan (the teen-ager) will make up the lunches for everyone the night before. No more "emergency" demands will be permitted in the morning. Each child will take time in the evening to go over his plans for the next day, and see that everything is taken care of. Mother and Dad will get up a half hour earlier in the morning to have a quiet time of Bible reading and prayer, letting the peace of Christ take command of their thoughts and plans. And the entire family will gather for prayer before breakfast.

Thus the father brings the focus of the family to rest upon Christ, the source of their harmony and peace. He uses his authority not to lord it over his wife and children, but gently to build them up, teach them, encourage them, plan for them, and direct them.

Yet his authority is not without the firmness, even the sternness, of Christ either. Where the do-it-yourself father might become lax or uncertain of himself, the father living under Christ is firm and unyielding. It is never a question in his household what the family will do Sunday morning. They are together in church, worshiping God. The father permits no breach of honesty or clean speech in his home. The obedience of the children is not a "sometime" thing. It is a settled issue, because Christ expects it.

The atmosphere in our home changed overnight when my wife and I came to see that discipline (spanking, when necessary) was not our thing but God's. A spanking is not a father inflicting his will on the child. It is the father's obedient response to God's Word, upon encountering rebellion or disobedience in a child. When we saw this, *spankings became harder, more consistent—and far less frequent!* Discipline carried out in obedience to a moral law which is applicable to both father and child has a different spiritual and emotional tone to it than discipline which is merely an expression of the father's personal will. And the child is quick to sense the difference. He is more responsive to the discipline, because it is operating through God's chain-of-command. A father who knows his standing under Christ will not hesitate to exercise firm discipline where it is needed, in order that Christ's will for the family come to practical realization.

3. Headship provides love.

The third component of headship is *love*. A Christian father does not lord it over his family, as head of the house. He uses that position as a base from which to *serve* his wife and children. This does not mean he becomes their servant, in the sense that he moves this way and that at their bidding, trying to please them and satisfy all their desires. The father serves them *by accepting the responsibility of being head of the house*. He serves them by working well at his trade or profession, in order to provide for their material needs. He serves them by taking time to give them the kind of leadership and direction which will knit them together and build them up as a family and as individuals. He serves them by earnestly becoming more and more disciplined to Christ. He serves them by encouraging their intellectual and artistic potential. He serves them by taking command and, with them, setting realistic goals which concur with God's word and God's will. Accordingly, the Christian father serves his family by *providing for them*—physically, emotionally, socially, intellectually, culturally, and spiritually. This is the kind of love Jesus taught us to expect from God, the model of all fatherhood. He gives us daily bread ... He protects us from evil ... He brings us into the Kingdom.

A MATE

Central to an understanding of the husband-wife relationship is the recognition that it makes up part of God's chain-of-command. "The head of every man is Christ, the head of a woman is her husband, and the head of Christ is God" (I Corinthians 11:3). As regards headship, the relationship between a husband and wife exactly parallels the relationship between the Father and Son. Once this fact is clearly established, mountains of confusion and misunderstanding begin to melt away.

Consider the relationship between the Father and the Son. The Son is subject to the Father, yet is equal with the Father. In purely human relationships, subjection often carries with it the stigma of inferiority. Not so in a Christian marriage. It is formed on a better model. Husband and wife are one, as the Father and Son are one. The wife is fully equal to the husband, as Christ is equal to God; yet she remains submissive to her husband in all things, as the Son is submissive in all things to the Father.

Equality and submission, far from being opposed to one another, are actually two sides of the same coin. In the Lord, it is neither a degradation of one, nor an exaltation of the other, but answers to the nature of both. In a Christian marriage, you cannot have one without the other. If a wife loses her submission to her husband, she loses her unity with him. If a husband abdicates his responsibility as head, he strikes at the very core of the relationship which God has established between him and his wife.

The Father exalts the Son. He delights to lift Him up, to honor Him. *This is the way headship behaves when it is grounded in love.* The courtesy which a husband shows toward his wife, the way he honors her before the children, his open and evident esteem for her, is the foundation upon which the wife's respect and trust in her husband is built. And then she, in turn, will acknowledge and exalt her husband, gladly submitting to his authority—as Jesus exalts the Father and submits to His authority.

American women today are not subjugated and oppressed, in need of "liberation." How anyone could grow up in our culture during the past 40 years and arrive at such a notion is incomprehensible. It is precisely the *absence* of male authority which plagues American culture. Husbands and fathers have abdicated their responsibility. We are fast becoming a matriarchal society. The teaching and discipline of the children, responsibility for the upkeep and management of the home, the family image in the community, participation in church and civic affairs and, increasingly, major responsibility for the financial support of the family—all of this has been laid on the women's shoulders. Small wonder that she begins to voice some complaint! But we live in an age when values and understanding have become so twisted out of shape that the remedy being offered is more of the same! More opportunities for women to take on the responsibilities of men—like a runner panting to the finish line of a mile run, and being told to elbow into the starting line for a two-mile run.

Women who work at a trade or profession certainly deserve to be paid in relation to what they produce, without regard to their sex. But such considerations, while not unimportant, are nevertheless peripheral to the central factors which are upsetting family relationships. Despite the anti-house-wife, anti-motherhood, anti-marriage propaganda being spewed out today, a majority of women will still end up getting married and having children. No amount of tinkering with employment practices and such like will get at the root of the problem which American women are facing.

The problem is mass abdication on the part of the husband. The need in American families today is not some kind of manufactured "equality" between husband and wife. The equality is already there, God-given, waiting to be discovered. The need is for *headship*. Let men accept the responsibility of being head of the family, and wives will find a freedom, a liberation, under their authority such as no constitutional amendment could ever guarantee.

A MAP

The goal of a Christian family is to glorify God by projecting into the world a demonstration of His Kingdom. The family is meant to be a living parable of heavenly realities and relationships.

How may the family reach this goal? How can father and mother and children so live together that those who see them and know them will be able to say, "Now, there is a bit of heaven on earth!" The Bible sets down no less a goal than this for the family—"heaven on earth" (Deuteronomy 11:21). And it maps out the course by which this goal can be reached: "You shall lay up these words of mine in your heart and in your soul . . . and you shall teach them to your children, talking of them when you are sitting in your house, and when you are walking by the way, and when you lie down, and when you rise" (Deuteronomy 11:18-19).

The Word of God—this is a father's map. As he applies this Word to the life of his family, they will be able to move on a steady course through the storms of our time toward God's appointed goal. The father's role at this point is basically twofold. He is *prophet*, in that he presents God to his family; he is *priest*, in that he presents his family to God.

The religious training which God expects a father to give his children is no "lick-and-a-promise." It is a *diligent* teaching. "And these words which I command to you this day shall be upon your heart; and you shall teach them *diligently* to your children" (Deuteronomy 6:6-7). Not in a harsh, oppressive, school-master spirit. But, rather, a quiet threading of God's Word, and God's Spirit, into the warp and woof of family life—"when you sit in the house, when you are out for a walk, when you are in bed, when you get up" (Deuteronomy 6:7). God's Word becomes a natural point-of-reference for anything that may come up in the family. And, through the Word, Jesus takes up His dwelling in the family—as naturally as the sunlight streams through the window when the shade is pulled aside.

It is this presence of Jesus which is the goal of a father's teaching. The teaching is diligent because His presence in the family is important—surpassingly important. We live in an age when a thousand sirens beckon for the ears and minds of our children. It is not enough to teach them a code of ethics. It is not enough to teach them a few rote prayers. Our homes must be so filled with the presence of Jesus that they encounter Him at every turn, come to know Him as effortlessly as they come to know their parents. In such a setting Jesus can engage their loyalty and fire their imagination. And this is the only antidote to the powers of darkness and corruption which are loose in the world today. The time is past when parents can give their children a pleasant surface-coating of religion. Our children are either going to be filled with Jesus and excited about Him, or filled with sin and excited about it. All that we can bring our children will be worthless unless we can bring them Jesus.

How many fathers, even Christian fathers, take seriously their prophetic role in the family? How many can stand before God and say, "I have taught them your word"? Who brings the children to Sunday School? *Mother!* Who takes the lead in family devotions? *Mother!* Who prays with the children as they go to bed? *Mother!* The greatest single cause of decline in home and church is that *men have abdicated as spiritual leaders.* By their life and example, they have successfully conveyed to their sons that religion is essentially "women's business." This has prompted one Bible teacher to say that the greatest single result of a religious awakening in our day would be the transfer of spiritual authority and responsibility back to men.*

A father's priestly role is a natural counterpart to his prophetic role. Through prayer and intercession he presents his family to God. Here it is important to recognize the *spiritual authority* which God invests in one called to be a "priest." His prayers have power because God has charged him with certain responsibility. He dare not evade this responsibility through any feelings of false modesty. The primary responsibility rests with the father —then with the mother, should the father be absent from the home. Called to be a priest unto his family, the father must come reverently, yet boldly, before God and present each family member before His presence. The father who undergirds and surrounds his family with his powerful intercessions has established the family's well-being on immovable granite.

The prayers which we teach our children are integral to Christian family life; they bring the child into personal contact with God. But they cannot become a substitute or replacement for the father's priestly prayers. His prayers are invested with special authority for the provision and protection of his family.

---

* From a talk by Derek Prince. The writer acknowledges his debt to Mr. Prince for a number of the insights in this article.

The role of priestly intercessor requires a *disciplined prayer life.* Like a marksman with a rusty rifle, like an archer with an unstrung bow, is the father-priest with a slipshod prayer life. He who has little intimacy with God will secure few blessings for his family.

We live in a time of great moral and spiritual upheaval, a stormy time. Storms are not times for polite or inconsequential conversation, and so this is direct and to the point: *Father, the responsibility for the direction of the family is in your hands.* As you take the wheel, and stand at your station, God will stand with you. And you will guide your family into "days of heaven upon earth!"

If you have enjoyed this little booklet . . . you may be interested in knowing that there is further help and instruction concerning God's plan for marriage and the family.

Pastor Christenson has written an entire book on the subject entitled, *The Christian Family*. This marvelous presentation of the divine order for proper family life has helped many thousands of people across America in their quest for a happy home.

And you might find the *Study Guide*, designed to be used with the book itself, helpful for in-depth consideration of the vital issues pertaining to satisfactory relationships.

There is also available a set of eleven supplementary cassettes by Rev. Christenson which we would heartily recommend.

These additional aids can be purchased at your local bookstore, or from Bethany Fellowship, Inc., 6820 Auto Club Road, Minneapolis, MN 55438.

THE CHRISTIAN FAMILY—$4.95
STUDY GUIDE—95¢
SET OF CASSETTES—$39.95